Jim the Gymnast

Written by Sally Cole
Illustrated by Suzie Byrne

Jimmy the gymnast looked down at all the children. They all looked so small. Jimmy held on by one finger and waved to them. He was right at the top of the highest wall. Anyone else would have been scared but not Jimmy the gymnast.

There was no one who could do gymnastics like Jimmy. He could do cartwheels and somersaults and never stop in between. He could jump, and swing, and leap, and roll. Everyone said he was fantastic at gymnastics.

Jimmy's dad said, "That boy must be part frog or he's eaten a jumping bean!"

Jimmy's dad was a window cleaner. He cleaned the windows on the highest skyscrapers in town. He went up and down the skyscrapers on a platform. Jimmy wanted to be a window cleaner, just like his dad.

But his dad said, "You can't be a window cleaner, you never keep still. You're a jumping bean!"

One day, Dad said, "Jimmy would you like to come to work with me? We'll be high up and you'll be able to see all over the town. But no gymnastics from you!"

"Wow, that would be so cool," Jimmy said.

The next morning it was raining, but Dad said it'd be all right for them to go. Jimmy and Dad put on their hard hats and fixed their safety harnesses to the platform. Up, up, up they went, to the top of the skyscraper. It was a very long way up, and Jimmy could see all over town.

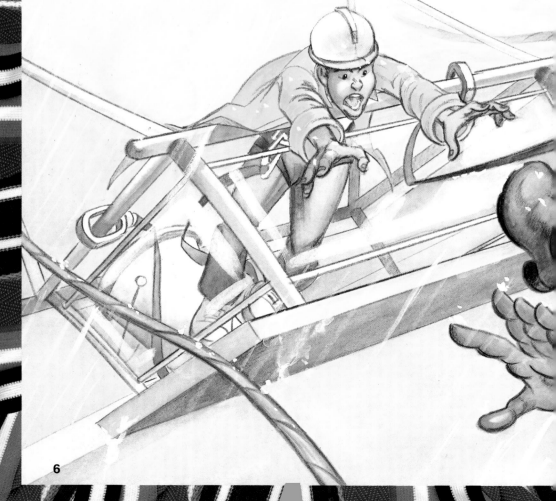

As they got to the top of the building, the wind started to blow very hard. Dad leaned over to clean a window. As he reached out, a gust of wind hit the platform. Dad slipped and fell over the side. He caught his foot in the rope and was left swinging upside down.

"Help me! Help me, Jimmy!" Dad shouted.

Jimmy looked up and down the skyscraper. There was an open window above them and a closed window below them. The platform was shaking and jumping about in the wind. Jimmy was scared. Only one person could save Dad and that was him.

Jimmy knew he'd have to do something. He tried to pull Dad up onto the platform, but Dad was too heavy. Jimmy couldn't lower the platform because the rope was around Dad's foot. Jimmy tried shouting but the wind was so strong that no one could hear him. Jimmy had to get help, but how?

"Hang on, Dad, I'm going to use one of my gymnastic jumps to reach the open window," Jimmy shouted.

Jimmy looked up at the open window. He took a deep breath. Then he bent his knees and bounced gently up and down. With a big leap, Jimmy shot up in the air. He grabbed the edge of the window, scraping his fingers and making them bleed.

The blood was making Jimmy's fingers slip but he knew this was his only chance. Jimmy threw himself in the window and crashed onto the floor.

Jimmy was safe, but what about Dad? Dad was still hanging. Jimmy ran down the stairs, three at a time. He raced into the room below and threw open the window.

"Hold on, Dad, I'm going to get you," Jimmy shouted loudly.

Dad was still swinging in the wind, and the rope was still dangling. Jimmy leaned out as far as he could and grabbed for the rope. On his third try, he got it. Jimmy tugged and pulled at the rope.

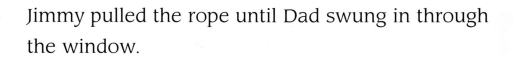

Jimmy pulled the rope until Dad swung in through the window.

"Jimmy the gymnast," Dad said, hugging Jimmy. "You saved my life. You are the best jumping-bean boy in the world."

The next morning the newspapers had photos of Jimmy and Dad. The headline said *Jimmy the Gymnast Saves His Dad* and underneath it said, *The Best Jumping-Bean Boy in the World*.